My Lord's Prayer

A PRAYER OF THANKS

by

Jean Webb

Spontaneous
Life
Publishing

ISBN: 978-1-7398954-3-3

Spontaneous
Life
Publishing

SpontaneousLife.net/Publishing

For anyone whose mind is open.

Contents

Lord's Prayer
Traditional Version

Our Father,

who art in heaven,

hallowed be thy name;

thy kingdom come;

thy will be done;

on earth as it is in heaven.

Give us this day our daily bread.

And forgive us our trespasses,

as we forgive those who trespass against us.

And lead us not into temptation;

but deliver us from evil.

For thine is the kingdom,

the power and the glory,

for ever and ever.

Amen.

Introduction

You only find out how much, or how little, you understand a thing when you try to explain it to someone else.

Teaching a child to pray is not an easy feat. The idea that all prayers are answered, and you can ask God for anything you want, can elicit a delighted response. There then follows a number of caveats. There's no use praying for the ability to fly, for example. Praying for material things isn't really what it's about, and praying for things your parents don't want you to have, such as a bunny or a hamster, is unlikely to get you anywhere.

One time a friend's cat went missing. Having assured my children that if you want something you should pray for it, they suggested we pray for the safe return of the cat. And so we prayed, every night, for Gus. After about 2 weeks of praying, I was starting to get a bit unsure of how to proceed. Chances were, the cat was probably decaying in a hedgerow somewhere, and would never be found. I was starting to suggest that, maybe, on this occasion Gus had gone to a better place and it was possible he wouldn't be seen again. And then, against all the odds, the cat appeared, slightly thin and scruffy-looking, but very much alive. My daughters were delighted. I was over the moon.

Then a friend got ill. My daughters had met her and loved her. They suggested we pray for her. We prayed for her every night. Until she died.

Another friend got ill. This time I decided to go one step further and asked her if I could pray with her, which provided a lovely bonding moment.

She died too.

Were our prayers not heard? Did our prayers not matter? It was around this time that my children's approach to prayer became somewhat more sceptical. I struggled to justify the importance and relevance of prayer, maybe I didn't understand it myself.

Another moment that caused reappraisal of prayer was when I read that Pope Francis wants to amend the translation of the Lord's Prayer.

The Lord's Prayer is central to the Christian religion. Whereas much of the foundations on which Christianity is built, for example the Nicene Creed, were put together centuries after the time of Jesus, the Lord's Prayer uses words that Jesus himself taught his disciples to say.

How surprising, then, that Pope Francis, in the 21st century, should suggest that we've had the translation of it slightly wrong all these years. In fact, he's managed to get a change approved, at least in Italian, if not in English.

The line that has been under scrutiny is "Lead us not into temptation". The point raised is why we should be asking God to "Lead us not into temptation" when God would never lead us into temptation. The approved change is for the translation to be "Do not let us fall into temptation," which many say is a better translation of the original text, being closer to the meaning of the verb used.

Not everyone agrees with this, as you might imagine. It calls into question the kind of God you believe in. Is the God of whom Jesus speaks one who would tempt us to evil? Pope Francis says not, and many share that view.

For me the surprise is that nobody ever raised the issue before. When it's pointed out it seems so obvious. The fact that it is being disputed in some quarters is to be expected, being so ingrained in our learning over so many generations. It made me question, though, whether this could lead to a more significant rethinking of the Lord's Prayer.

Having studied Greek, I decided to start with taking the prayer line by line, to see what I could find. Perhaps it would give me some ideas that might also help me with my other questions about prayer.

The approach I take in analysing the Lord's Prayer is to be as open-minded and unprejudiced as possible. I want to see everything anew through fresh eyes. I don't want to be confined by what would be acceptable to people I know through church, or what might be the generally held Christian view.

I attempt to relate the teachings within the Lord's Prayer to examples from my life, hoping that my interpretation is helpful to others.

Jean Webb, February 2022

Why Pray?

Prayer is defined as "the act or ceremony of speaking to God or a god, esp. to express thanks or to ask for help."[1]

If we say the object of religion is to find a way to be close to God, then speaking with God is key. This goes beyond organised religion, this applies to anyone who has faith in a creative force or a spiritual realm.

Jesus came to help us with our relationship with God. He came to overturn some of the religious traditions that had deviated from a focus on the God of Love.

The Lord's Prayer is the way that Jesus taught us to pray. It can be found in Matthew, chapter 6, with a shorter version in Luke, chapter 11. In Luke, Jesus is answering a question from one of the disciples: "Lord, teach us to pray". In Matthew, however, there is context to understand.

The teaching on how to pray in Matthew comes after Jesus has explained that it's important to carry out charitable acts in private, without fuss, unlike the hypocrites, who "call attention to their acts of charity"[2].

Jesus then follows with some do's and don'ts of prayer[3]. We shouldn't pray like the hypocrites "who love to pray publicly where everyone can see them", instead, Jesus says "pray to your Father in private".

---

[1] dictionary.cambridge.org
[2] Matthew 6:2
[3] Matthew 6:5-8

Also, we shouldn't be like the Gentiles who "think their prayers are answered merely by repeating their words again and again", for "your Father knows exactly what you need even before you ask him!".

When I read this passage in Matthew it makes me reappraise the approach to prayer I've known throughout my life.

Different churches have different approaches to prayer. Some go for the totally spontaneous, open invitation to all, to lead the congregation in prayers as they feel the urge. Other churches, or other parts of church services, are rather more scripted.

It feels to me that at some point the concept of praying together, which is a good thing ("For where two or three gather together as my followers, I am there among them", Matthew 18:20), could become praying publicly for the benefit of others.

Perhaps the part that stands out for me the most, though, is "your Father knows exactly what you need even before you ask him!" Through my life my prayers have rarely strayed from "please can I" or "please will You" in some form or other. Yet this sentence suggests God already knows what we want, so why should we ask?

The German theologian, Meister Eckhart[4], suggests that "If the only prayer you ever said was thank you, that

---

[4] For more information on Meister Eckhart see www.eckhartsociety.org

would be enough". When I first read this I found it puzzling – but what about all the things I want?

A prayer of thanks has many benefits. It calls us to, literally, count our blessings. It encourages gratitude, satisfaction with what we have, appreciation of "a glass half full".

A prayer of requests can be a focus on what we don't have, "a glass half empty". Underneath a request there is often lurking the thought process "I'll be happy if…", or "I'll be happy when…".

We're told in Matthew 7:7: "Ask and it will be given to you" (New International Version). This is to say that God is always ready and willing to help us in any way, with anything, we just need to ask.

We are defined by our free will, and we can choose to go it alone in every aspect of life and do the best that we can do. Or, we can proceed with continual reference to God, for what we want to achieve and how to achieve it.

The key point, I believe, is that we need to remind ourselves, through asking, who it is that is granting our requests, and what wonderful things we are given.

Asking for something, where you have faith your prayer will be answered, is one small step from thanking. I ask, secure in the knowledge that you will give me what I need, therefore I thank you in advance.

I don't believe that this prayer, the most important of prayers, taught by Jesus himself, is meant as a wish list

of outlandish requests. In this prayer, we're not asking
for anything other than what we know God wants for us.

Could it be interpreted more as a prayer of thanks?

Analysis

I've taken each line in Greek and translated the words literally. My desire has been to consider this with fresh eyes, but inevitably other influences have been brought to mind. I've used a combination of context, other bible references, different teachings and what you might call "intuitive input" to put forward new words that carry more meaning for me.

I find there's a wealth of treasure to be uncovered in each line.

I use Matthew 6 as the basis for analysis, with reference to Luke 11.

I make extensive use of the website biblehub.com for the original Greek, using the Nestle Greek New Testament 1904.

Unless otherwise stated, bible quotes in English are taken from the New Living Translation.

Our Father

> Πάτερ ἡμῶν
> Pater hemon
> Father of us

In the first word of the English translation we have a potential contradiction to consider, given the context. Use of the word "Our", or "of us", might seem to suggest that we should pray this prayer together, which would be at odds with Matthew 6:6 where Jesus suggests we should close the door and pray in secret.

Luke offers no help with this, in fact Luke 11:2 just has "Pater", "Father", not "of us"

Could it be that the use of "of us" in Matthew points to an emphasis not on us all speaking together, rather a reminder that we all share the same father?

If we believe in God, the God that Jesus talks about, then we believe that God created everything, and is the source of all life.

Therefore "of us" means "of all of us". We all share the same father. Whether we look like each other, whether we have anything in common, regardless of whether we ever meet, we were all created the same way.

We are created in God's image[5], just as we resemble our human father. I used to think that meant that God looks like us, with eyes, ears and a nose. Now I think that what created us is the God of Love and we have that same love inside us all.

---

[5] Genesis 1:27

Jesus teaches us about love. Comparing God to a parent is illustrating that love. We can relate the love that God has for us to the love that we have for our children, or our parents, and the love that they have for us.

We talk of 'Mother Earth', so why should God be a Father? Is it a reflection of the patriarchy? Does father command more respect?

I believe there's sufficient evidence elsewhere in the gospels to suggest that Jesus saw beyond gender. There are strong female characters, perhaps surprisingly so given the status of women in society at the time.

I don't think it is of material consequence which pronouns are used in relation to God. God is neither male nor female, God just is. It is to illustrate the love of God, and the fact that God is a giver of life, that God can be thought of as a parent. A male parent, particularly at the time of Jesus, would have been the more powerful, and Jesus talks of a God who is both loving and powerful, hence the use of "Father".

How meaningful is a prayer that simply says "God, you are my Father". More meaningful still is the prayer "God, you are Father of all of us".

Is there an element of thanks in this address? I think so. Thanks and respect. I see it as an expression of the vastness and the loving nature of God.

An interpretation I like of "Our father" is:

Giver of life to us all.

Who Art in Heaven

> ὁ ἐν τοῖς οὐρανοῖς
> Ho en tois ouranois
> The one in the heavens

This is in Matthew but not in Luke.

There is no verb here, it literally means, in reference to our father, "the one in the heavens". The word is plural, heavens, rather than the common translation, Heaven.

This is not an earthly father, who can only love us as much as a human can, this is the father who abides in Heaven, who is without limit. This is like the address on the envelope, this makes it specific that we're talking to someone other-wordly, non-human.

And where is heaven, or where are the heavens? Where does the envelope get delivered to?

The simple answer is we don't know. It used to be thought of as "up there", (pointing to the sky). This was before we'd explored the "heavens" and understood the concept of stars, galaxies and the wider universe. Presumably the pluralisation refers to the fact that the sky changes over time, so it was thought that there were multiple heavens above us, rather than us being given a glimpse of different parts of a constantly moving universe.

We now know that there is a vastness that exists outside our earth that is beyond our imagining. What we also know, from quantum physics, is that there is a vast emptiness within everything. That which is matter is a tiny portion of every atom. What is important, therefore, is not the material substance but the energy that moves the substance.

To my mind, it's in this vastness, within or without, that we find God. I see God as a form of energy. It is everywhere. It is potential beyond limit.

What is the aim of life? Surely it's to be with our heavenly Father? Does this mean in death, when we drop our earthly body? Or does it mean during life when we manage to feel close to our Father?

There's a kind of bliss that can be experienced in life that gives us an idea of what it would be to be in heaven. It's a spirit-soaring, deeply-felt joy, which is above all other pleasure, though it may only be felt in a fleeting moment. It's there for us whenever we can totally put aside our earthly troubles and focus on pure love. It may come from focusing on God, or love for another person, or admiration for a view, or musical sound. It is pure love, peace, ecstasy. This, I believe, is what it would be like to be where our Father is. This is a taste of what we want after we die, but it's something that's within reach whilst we're alive.

Heaven would seem to me to be a word that describes a state rather than a place. God gives us access to that state.

Where Heaven is You are.

Hallowed be Thy Name

Ἁγιασθήτω τὸ ὄνομά σου
Hagiastheto to onoma sou
Hallowed be the name of you

This is the same in Matthew and Luke.

The word hallow means to "make holy", or "honour as holy", therefore this could be translated as "Let Your name be honoured as holy". Holy means "having a spiritually pure quality" or "entitled to worship" [6].

The verb is passive, it references "your name" (object) but there is no subject, nobody named as doing the honouring.

It is reasonable to imply that we are the ones that should honour God as holy, or to worship God.

Why do we need to worship God? Does God need our worship?

No, we need to worship God because we need to constantly remind ourselves that there is a power greater than us, instead of thinking of ourselves as a single lone individual, an ego. If we kid ourselves that we're in charge, that we can control the things that happen around us, then we'll be like King Canute sitting asking the waves to stay back. God is in charge. God can make things happen. Our task, minute by minute, is to recognise our place in relation to God.

God does not need us to honour what He is, God has no ego that needs to be inflated. We need to recognise God's role in relation to ours, for ourselves.

---

[6] Definitions from dictionary.com

I find it interesting that the word "name" is used (onoma). We should honour God's *name*. Why the emphasis on name, why not "we should honour God"?

A name is something we call people, therefore I think the emphasis is on the act of "calling", or on us as the "callers". I think there's a distinction to be made between a child calling on his or her human parent, and any of us calling on God.

My children might call to me from another room and ask me something. I may or may not hear, depending on the volume of the tv or any music that's playing, and depending on whether I'm doing something that interferes with my ability to hear them – talking on the phone or boiling the kettle perhaps. As earthly parents we don't always hear, but God always hears. All of us, all the time. When we call to God we don't have to shout above the background noise, we are always heard. Even if we all call at the same split second, there is no limit, there is no waiting in line.

This is what sets our relationship with God apart from other relationships, and makes time spent talking to God holy, unlike any other conversation.

The clarity of the response or the answer to our prayer might not seem so obvious, that depends on the level of background noise we generate around us, but our prayers are always heard.

The relationship each of us has with God is unique, personal, and not shared. If one person needs me for something then I am temporarily unavailable to another. God, on the other hand, is available to each of us, in whatever way needed, all the time. This is hard to imagine. It's as if each of us has our own private God, available to us 24x7. Yet we all share the same God.

God's power cannot be used up, in fact it can seem that the more power you use, the more you get. The power that's available is beyond measure and beyond comprehension.

The resistance to that power is what we need to concern ourselves with. If you think of a hosepipe that allows water to gush along it, it's possible to stand on the pipe, slowing or stopping the flow. It's the same with a blood vessel or an electric cable – if the transport mechanism is compromised then it all goes wrong.

What can happen when we're anxious or scared, though, is that we can squeeze onto this cable or pipe and, in gripping so tightly, stop the flow. The hardest thing when you're scared is to relax, but in relaxing and being calm, with a call to God, we allow God's goodness to flow freely to us.

Our earthly bodies are potential transport mechanisms for God. If we allow God's power to course through us then we can amaze, delight and empower ourselves and those around us.

The glory is God's. If we take off the veil we've been hiding under, wipe the windscreen that's been obscuring our view, step off the hosepipe, unravel the cable, we can connect with that power. We just need to call God's name.

We call Your Holy name.

Thy Kingdom Come

> Ἐλθέτω ἡ βασιλεία σου
> Eltheto he basileia sou
> Come the kingdom of you

This is the same in Matthew and in Luke.

The word "come" has the sense of "draw near". It refers to the kingdom.

What is God's kingdom? A kingdom is ruled by a king, therefore God's kingdom is ruled by God. But isn't everywhere ruled by God anyway? There seems to be a distinction being drawn between what is God's and what is ours. Perhaps the kingdom of heaven is God's, and 'the world', with all its imperfections, is ours.

Luke 17:21 says that "the kingdom of God is within you". Does this mean heaven is within us all? Does it mean we can all access heaven? Does it mean that the kingdom of God is something we can reach individually, rather than waiting collectively for the kingdom of God to come to us all?

I used to think this line was referring to the fact that one day God's kingdom would come to everyone all at once. Now I wonder if it means that we should focus on connecting with God, approaching God's kingdom, or finding the kingdom of God that is within us.

The verb is a command requiring immediate response. It isn't a future tense or a statement of what will happen at some later date, it's referring to the here and now.

I don't think we're asking for God's kingdom to come "one day", this is for immediate action. "God, come to me now", or since God never left, perhaps the onus is on us to draw near to God.

Let us draw near to You

Thy Will be Done, on Earth as it is in Heaven

Γενηθήτω τὸ θέλημά σου, Ὡς ἐν οὐρανῷ, καὶ ἐπὶ γῆς
Genetheto to thelema sou, Hos en ourano, kai epi ges
Be done the will of you, as in heaven, also on earth

This is the same in Matthew and in Luke.

"Be done" is in the third person and is passive, therefore an action for it (the will) to be done, on earth as it is in heaven.

Even the most egotistical of us would concede that we can't make things happen in heaven. God is synonymous with heaven. Heaven is the aim, it is 'with God'. Who makes things happen on earth? We do. We make daily, hourly, minute by minute decisions that affect our lives. We can ask God for help with these decisions, and they can be according to, or against, the will of God, as far as we can ascertain what the will of God is. The choice is ours. We have to first establish what God's will is, in any given situation, and then we have to do our bit to carry it out.

In heaven, everything is God's. Since God is Love then that means that in heaven there is nothing but love and peace and harmony. What we want is for that same love, peace and harmony on earth, that is God's will. By praying 'thy will be done' we are asking for more of Heaven's goodness around us on earth.

You could say that it is the aim for us and for our lives, that we do our bit to make Earth more like Heaven. We do this by carrying out God's will.

If we think that anything other than God's will is going to make us happy in the long run, we are mistaken. If our heart's desire is something material or physical, or something that gives us status or power, we will at some point find that the happiness these things brought us is shallow and short lived. Whereas if our will is aligned with God's will for us, it's like swimming with the current and we're lifted along the path of life.

We have the ability to tune into God's will. It's not easy, it's not always clear, but, with practice and dedication, understanding God's will in any given situation is something we can get better at. We can learn to recognise when we get it right by listening to the feeling we have deep down inside when we know something to be true.

This is a pledge, it is the point of these first few lines. We've identified who we're talking to (Giver of life to us all), where to find this giver of life (where Heaven is You are), we've called to God (we call Your holy name) and expressed a need to be close to God, (let us draw near to You). Now we deliver the first punch line:

We want to carry out Your will.

Give Us this Day our Daily Bread

> Τὸν ἄρτον ἡμῶν τὸν ἐπιούσιον δὸς ἡμῖν σήμερον
>
> Ton arton hemon ton epiousion dos hemin semeron
>
> The bread of us daily give us today

This is the same in Matthew and Luke except for the word for "today" which is slightly different, but essentially means the same[7].

This is the second use of the word "hemin", though in a slightly different form, meaning "us". Does the use of "us" mean we should pray this prayer together after all, despite the context being about praying in private?

The bread we're referring to is quite specifically "daily bread". It is a way of saying "the food we need today". It doesn't imply "all the food we might wish for", or "the finest food and lots of it", rather "the food we need to keep us sustained."

The mood of the verb used suggests that this is a request. "Please can we have the food we need today".

Bearing in mind "Your Father knows exactly what you need before you ask him", as well as the suggestion we should pray in private, I'd like to consider whether this could be anything other than a request.

We come across the same question for the next few lines. On the face of it, the things we are asking God to do are:

---

[7] Luke uses the word καθ'ἡμέραν, kath'hemeran, which means "each day", as opposed to σήμερον, semeron, "today"

> *Give us* our daily bread
> *Forgive us* our trespasses
> *Lead us* not into temptation
> *Deliver us* from evil.

The words that are key here are the verbs. In these four lines they are imperative, "Do this!", with a sense of urgency – "Do this now!".

In the Appendix you'll find a fuller analysis of the verbs used in the prayer, exploring the finer points of grammar.

It strikes me that the issue Pope Francis has raised about "Lead us not into temptation" could also be applied to these other lines in the same way. God would not lead us into temptation. God will always deliver us from evil. God forgives us our trespasses. God can be relied upon to give us what we need when we need it, which is what is meant by our daily bread.

Why do we need to ask, since God knows what we need? If we don't ask, do we not get?

Or do we need to ask to remind ourselves where things come from?

We could think of this prayer as a kind of contract, a statement of who does what. In the same way that a project manager assigns roles and gives out instructions: "brick-layers, lay the bricks; carpenters, do the woodwork" etc, we're saying "God, give us our daily bread, forgive us" and so on. Then, elsewhere in the prayer, we find the part we must play: we must carry out

God's will and we must forgive those who trespass against us.

Thinking about this in relation to a human father, a child might consider the role of a parent saying:

"Give me food, clothes and a roof over my head. Teach me, encourage me, support me, love me, care for me."

Most parents would say "Of course I'll do these things, it's what I do!"

This is subtly different from:

"You always make sure I have food to eat, clothes to wear and a roof over my head. You teach me right from wrong, you encourage me in my education. You always give me the support I need. You love me and care for me."

The words "thank you" aren't included but they're very obviously implied.

The same is true with God. The fact that He gives me the food I need each day is worthy of acknowledgement, but is it a request?

Another clue, perhaps, is the use of the word "us". Is the prayer saying "Please give those of us praying our daily bread"? Or is it saying "Please give everyone you created their daily bread"? Or could it be "You give us all our daily bread (thank you)"?

Ultimately, I believe, the important question is who does the giving? God does the giving. The prayer is a reminder that, as we know from elsewhere in the bible

"All things come from You"[8]. All the bread, all the food, all the sustenance we need, comes from You.

When we call God's holy name, we should feel confident that we'll be heard. If we put out there either a request or an assertion that God will give / does give us our daily bread, we should no longer worry about where the next bread is coming from.

There's also another point of context. At this point in time, people were being trained away from belief in many gods. The early followers of Jesus would have been swimming against the tide of popular belief in maintaining that there is only one God, who is the source of everything. Therefore maybe the point is that Jesus was emphasising that we entreat the same god for everything, for food, for forgiveness, and for the way forward.

As we say these words in the Lord's Prayer, we are bringing to mind the generosity of the one true God and therefore feeling gratitude.

In My Lord's Prayer I prefer to not use commands, instead I use statements. I think that the implied thanks are important, and it fits in the context of "your father knows what you need before you ask him."

If you ask someone for something, then you are also acknowledging that it's them that provides it.

An interpretation I like is:

---

[8] 1 Chronicles 29:14

Give Us this Day our Daily Bread

*It is You that gives us the sustenance we need
each day.*

And Forgive Us our Trespasses

Καὶ ἄφες ἡμῖν τὰ ὀφειλήματα ἡμῶν

Kai aphes hemin ta opheilemata hemon
And forgive us the debts of us

The need for forgiveness and absolution from sin forms an important part of all religions.

Aphes

The word "aphes" is commonly translated as "forgive", however it is also used in several other places in the bible to mean "allow" or "let be".

In terms of trespasses or sins, it could have a sense of "let go of", ie "allow us to let go of our sins".

When we approach God because we have something to apologise for, God lets us become unattached from those things we've done. Like a weight we've been carrying around, God takes the burden off us and lets us carry on our lives unencumbered.

The verb is a command, just as "Give", yet the same argument can be made for it to be a reminder of what God does, rather than necessarily a question. God takes away the baggage of what we have previously done.

Sins or Trespasses?

This is one of the sections where Matthew and Luke diverge a little.

In Matthew the word is "opheilemata", which is commonly translated to mean debts, whereas in Luke the word is "hamartias", which means "failures, faults, sins". It is possible that the original Aramaic word used could have been *ḥôbâ*, which can mean "debt" or "sin"[9].

In the time of Jesus, a sin or a failure might result in a debt, in the form of a sacrifice. To do wrong, therefore, is to incur a debt.

I was brought up with the traditional version of the prayer, using the word "trespass", rather than "sin". I like the word trespass. It suggests you've lost your way a little and ended up walking across a field that doesn't have a public right of way.

The things I tend to ask forgiveness for are usually when I've not deliberately set out to do something wrong, I've just allowed myself to be caught up in the moment. I may have been attracted by the wrong priorities, done something to please someone and ignored the little voice inside that suggested this might not be the best idea. I can think of times when I've taken a risk that with hindsight wasn't the best, but I struggle to think of times when I've said to myself "I know this is absolutely the wrong thing to do but I'm going to do it anyway". I think that's true for most people, most of the time – we don't set out with ill intent but, somehow or other, we occasionally end up on the wrong path. This fits the description of "trespass".

---

[9]

www.academia.edu/35932158/Exegesis_of_the_Lords_Prayer

This won't be true for everyone. I've never robbed a bank or murdered someone, but there are plenty who have. At every fork in every road through life we make decisions which affect our future. Some people feel they have been led down a particular path, and they might feel, for whatever reason, that they have no choice in taking the wrong path. God sees all of this, and God forgives.

Recognising the wrong path

The issue, then, is less one of how we came to be on a given path, rather that we have a point where we recognise that we're going in the wrong direction.

If we say that the way to reach the North Pole is to travel north, then any time I travel south I am going the wrong way. This is the same with anything I do that doesn't take me towards love, peace and harmony – anything else takes me away from God, away from Heaven. You can still get to the North Pole by taking a detour southwards, it'll just take you that bit longer. You need to realise your mistake and then you can take a different turn.

If we don't realise our mistake then we keep going, potentially blissfully unaware that the direction we're heading in is not God's chosen way for us. There will hopefully come a point at which we take heed of signs that we might have been missing, and we recognise a wrong path for what it is.

Perceived vs Actual Sin

We only ask for forgiveness when we perceive a reason for it. That which we ask to be forgiven for depends on our perception. There may be things we may stand accused of, but if we don't recognise them as sins then we won't ask for forgiveness. It is when we perceive our guilt that we ask for forgiveness.

Likewise there are things that may leave us wracked with guilt – "if only I hadn't…". This might be something that wasn't technically our fault, or count as a sin in the traditional sense, but we can still feel guilty and ask for forgiveness from our perceived sin.

I have been accused, and admitted to, driving above the speed limit on more than one occasion. What are my feelings about these offences? I feel silly for having been caught – I should have been more aware of the presence of speed cameras – but I don't feel guilty. Have I repented to God? No. Being guilty of speeding when there were no consequences has not left me feeling guilty. Had there been consequences, had I been involved in an accident where someone was hurt, then of course I would feel guilt. Each time I've driven above the speed limit I've taken a risk, and, other than a speeding fine, I've got away with it.

Incidentally, the speed awareness course was an effective deterrent against speeding, so I am a more careful driver as a result, but I've never seen this issue as something I've had to put right with God.

The world, or the local constabulary at least, had me as guilty, but I didn't feel guilt.

I remember an occasion when I was at the kitchen sink on a Sunday afternoon, when my husband came up to me, put his arms around me and said "I'm sorry about earlier". My heart warmed at these words and I said "Don't worry, it's fine." We continued to talk and it very quickly transpired that the thing he was apologising for was not the thing I thought he should apologise for. What he was actually apologising for was something I'd barely even noticed, whereas the thing that I thought he should apologise for was something he defended as being right and he still stood by it. Instead of being a lovely make-up moment it degenerated into the continuation of an argument.

Our feelings of guilt often don't match others' perceptions and often don't follow any logic at all.

There are sociopaths who don't feel guilt for the most abhorrent crimes, and there are lovely, innocent people who live their lives plagued with a guilt that no-one else can understand. There's a world of difference between guilt in the eyes of others, including the lawmakers, and a feeling of guilt. Feeling guilt is entirely subjective.

Hearing the "inner no"

What things weigh on our hearts? Something we did that we shouldn't have done, or not done that we wish we'd done. Guilt. Shame. Regret.

Some things we do give us a deep feeling of happiness, a feeling of lightness, being right with God. When we have this feeling we know, deep down, that we've done the right thing. I call it the "inner yes".

Some things leave us unaffected – whether I buy the blue or the green, it doesn't really matter, neither affects me deeply.

Some things leave us feeling uneasy, or on a sliding scale from a little bit unsure to absolute dread or regret. These are the things that weigh on our hearts. This is what I call sin, it's an "inner no".

I don't refer to an external measure of right and wrong, or the way in which those around me might judge me, I refer to the inner compass, the "inner yes" or the "inner no". We need to know that we're forgiven, and released from the weight of those things that we find give us that "inner no".

Therefore sin, trespass, debt, or anything that we need to be set loose from, is simply anything that resulted in us following an "inner no" rather than an "inner yes". Sometimes the inner guidance system isn't clear, but when it becomes clear, and you realise you've not been on the right path, that's the point at which you feel guilt and you can change path.

What we need help with is in tuning in to our "inner no" before we do something that it's hard to recover from.

Absolute Right or Wrong

The more I think about it, the fewer examples of absolute right and wrong exist. I believe there is a "divine dichotomy" that means two things that would seem to be in opposition can both be right.

In football, a striker who is about to take a penalty might pray to score the goal, along with his team-mates and all of the supporters of his team. The goalkeeper might also be praying to save the goal, along with his team-mates and all the supporters of his team. The ground could be divided, half praying one way, the other half praying for the opposite.

Who is right? Who does God support?

God created both sets of players and all the fans, and wants all of them to be happy.

There are other examples in politics, for example. On binary either/or, yes/no questions, there might be excellent reasons to believe God would support either view. All we can do, when we get the chance to vote, is go with what we believe to be the truth as we see it. The fact that a friend or family member votes a different way means they have a different truth.

What is sin?

Going back to the first section of the Lord's Prayer, the aim, you could say, is for Earth to be more like Heaven.

The question, then, when considering sin and the need for forgiveness, is to ask whether this act, or this behaviour, or this mindset, will make Earth more like Heaven or not.

An alternative question would be "what would Love do?"

What does 1 Corithians 13 tell us about love:

> "Love is patient and kind. Love is not jealous or boastful or proud or rude. It does not demand its own way. It is not irritable, and it keeps no record of being wronged. It does not rejoice about injustice but rejoices whenever the truth wins out. Love never gives up, never loses faith, is always hopeful, and endures through every circumstance."

Therefore sin could be defined as including: impatience; being unkind, jealous, boastful, proud, rude; demanding our own way; being irritable; keeping a record of being wronged; rejoicing in injustice or untruth; giving up; losing faith; lacking hope and endurance.

This is a different way of thinking about sin. Living by this code is a challenge indeed. If I was tempted to feel self-satisfied about the fact I've never robbed a bank or murdered someone, when I look at this list I can see a few things I do on a regular basis that are unloving and take me on the wrong path.

This seems like an uncomfortably big stick for us to beat ourselves with. Yet I believe living like this is the best way to make Earth more like Heaven.

How does God forgive?

With such a list to live by, we could all be in need of forgiveness most of the time. But is anything we do ever unforgiveable in God's mind? I don't think so.

God gives second chances, then third, fourth, fifth, and so on. God wants us to become aware of the "inner no" and move towards the "inner yes". God doesn't want to punish us for the things we've done, rub our noses in it, feel the weight of His disappointment, God just wants to help us to the direction of Love.

God doesn't want us to carry around a burden of guilt. In fact, we can only be the best that we can be, and achieve what God wants for us, when we lose the burden of guilt.

Losing the feeling of guilt

What can we do to lose the feeling of guilt? We can't undo the past. We have to accept what has happened. We have to accept ourselves.

The idea is that we hold this thing before God and say "Let me not feel this burden". Once we've done this the burden can leave us. Before we gave it to God it weighed us down, affected our behaviour, but after we've given it to God we are set free.

God doesn't want us to feel guilty. That's why God forgives. Over and over again, God forgives.

If God forgives then what are we worried about? Why carry the guilt? How ridiculous then to say "Yes, but my partner/mum/friend/neighbour hasn't forgiven me!" Who is more important?

Steps to receive and accept forgiveness:

> Step 1 – Tune in to the "inner no", in terms of things that are in the past, or things we're currently doing. This might mean identifying the guilt we're holding onto, or the ways in which we believe we are currently straying from the path God has for us.

> Step 2 – Say "Forgive me." This means "Let me take a different path. Take this guilt away from me. Let me not feel this burden".

> Step 3 – Trust that we will have help in finding the way forward, and that the guilt has no place in our lives and is gone. Change thought patterns every time the old ways beckon, or whenever guilt tries to reappear.

All of these steps can be difficult to achieve.

I can think of things I've done in the past that I can admit were wrong. I remember once being difficult with someone at work and coming to the realisation later that the action I took, and the words I said, were unnecessarily harsh. This person left the job and I've never seen her since, so I've never had a chance to tell her I'm sorry. She probably thinks of me as a mean person, quite justifiably. I realise now I'd strayed down a path of self-importance at the time, and I was annoyed that she hadn't pandered to my ego. However, I've learned from this experience and whether or not she thinks ill of me, there's nothing to be gained by carrying around guilt in relation to this. So, I've identified the guilt, I've asked for it to be taken away, and now I have to remind myself that I'm not guilty, and any time the thought "I'm a bad person because…" comes into mind, I have to let go of it. I need to replace it with the certainty that I've handed it over, and now it has gone.

There is nothing to be gained by living in the past, obsessing over things that were done that might have been done better. We should focus on what is in front of us now. We should accept that God forgives us for anything that isn't helpful to the goal He has for us. We should lose the past, lose the guilt, and therefore free ourselves to be what we can be.

What if we don't say sorry?

What if we don't realise that something we did was wrong, unkind, rude, or otherwise unloving?

Are we still forgiven if we don't say sorry?

There's another use of the word "aphes" that is very often quoted, in Luke 23:34: "Father, forgive them, for they don't know what they are doing". It's exactly the same verb, used in the same way as here.

Is Jesus saying:

"Father, please forgive these people, regardless of whether they ever ask you to, because they don't understand what they are doing"?

or is he saying:

"Father, You forgive these people, just like You always forgive everyone, regardless of whether they ask You to, regardless of whether or not they understand what they are doing"?

I think God forgives without an apology. God just wants us to go the right way. An apology is useful to us, as an acknowledgement that we got it wrong, which leaves us more open to a change in direction in the future.

When we say the Lord's Prayer we aren't, at this point, listing those things that we need forgiveness for. We're not saying "sorry I got impatient and irritable ...", or "sorry I felt so fearful and alone..." or "sorry I felt like giving up...", this is a prayer that references <u>us</u>.

Either we're saying together "Please forgive all of us for all the things we do wrong, whatever they are", or we're saying:

You forgive us when we go wrong. You set us free from our guilt.

As We Forgive Those who Trespass against Us

> Ὡς καὶ ἡμεῖς ἀφήκαμεν τοῖς ὀφειλέταις
> ἡμῶν
> Hos kai hemeis aphekamen tois opheiletais
> hemon
> As we also should forgive the debtors of us

Matthew and Luke differ slightly here, though the meaning is very much the same. Luke says this:

> Καὶ γὰρ αὐτοὶ ἀφίομεν παντὶ ὀφείλοντι ἡμῖν
> Kai gar autoi aphiomen panti opheilonti hēmin
> Also for ourselves we forgive everyone indebted
> to us

Both versions are suggesting we should forgive others in the same way that God forgives us.

The way the Lord's Prayer tends to be recited can sound as if we're asking God to forgive us in the same way that we forgive others. Pity the world if God forgave in the same way that we do!

What do we need to forgive?

The wording is around debts, letting people off their debts. There's a sense of us feeling that someone owes us something. What might they owe us?

I'd suggest this is about an implied sense of fairness – "I'll be nice to you and you be nice to me". We might feel someone owes us a debt of gratitude, or kindness, or civility. Therefore, in this passage, we're saying "You don't owe me anything", or "I'll be nice to you regardless of how you are with me".

My behaviour, no matter how angelic I am, shouldn't lead me to expect anything from anyone else. Someone else's bad behaviour, no matter how bad, requires nothing of me.

Why should we forgive?

Other than "because Jesus told us to forgive", why else is forgiveness so important?

The answer is that not forgiving, or holding on to unforgiveness, distorts our thoughts and therefore our behaviour. We might take steps to avoid a person or a situation, or have a niggling feeling, like a tiny stone in our shoe that is a cause of intermittent pain, whenever we think of a particular situation.

Not forgiving harms <u>us</u>, it doesn't affect the person we aren't forgiving, it affects us.

Forgiving someone sets <u>us</u> free, not them.

If I pause to reflect on the opposite of love, I'd say it was unforgiveness. You might think it would be hate, but hate has a cause, and that cause is unforgiveness. I hate someone because I consider they've done me wrong, or done something I don't approve of, or they've disrespected me or shunned me, or whatever.

Not forgiving is the opposite of loving, it's keeping hold of an unloving thought and feeling justified in doing so.

Not forgiving is blocking the flow of love. Blocking love is the same as blocking God, putting up a barrier or a defence against all that is good for us.

"Yes but they need to learn" you might say. Whether or not the person learns that what they did had implications for others, or whether or not they moderate their behaviour, that is a matter for them. My forgiveness of others is a matter for me.

The best way to teach anybody anything is by example. A loving and forgiving example is better than a bitter, defensive one, surely.

The importance of forgiveness is given emphasis by being the one thing it's suggested *we* should pledge to do, within the Lord's Prayer, therefore it must be very important in our relationship with God.

Do not judge

What precedes the need to forgive is a feeling of being wronged. If I feel wronged by someone then I judge them harshly.

Who is it that is qualified to judge another? Who is it that sees all sides to any interaction, and sees past all misunderstandings? Not me. I am not the one that should be judging.

When I first read the New Testament from beginning to end I was struck by the constant repetitions of "Do not judge", Matthew 7:1 is one of many examples. I came away with a clear feeling that Jesus does not want us to judge each other. Unforgiveness is judgement plus a righteous feeling that our ill-feeling is justified, because "they are wrong". Unforgiveness suggests I'm right to not extend loving thoughts to someone.

Yet how unambiguous is the message, here in the Lord's Prayer, that we should forgive just as God does?

Having something to forgive someone for comes from first of all making a judgement. Better then to not make the judgement in the first place.

How does God forgive?

God forgives us every time we stray. Every time, even if we keep making the same mistake over and over again. Like the drug addict child who comes back to take money or steal from his or her family, only to disappear again then turn up months later and repeat the same pattern. God forgives, constantly, repeatedly.

As discussed earlier, I don't believe God needs an apology or a confession before He forgives us, and therefore, in that same way, we should forgive others.

Of course it's easier to forgive someone if they ask us to, and we can feel great resistance to the idea of forgiveness without an apology, but, I believe, the harder it is to forgive somebody, the more important it is that we should.

See it from their point of view

The simplest route to forgiveness is where a misunderstanding is uncovered. Rather than making assumptions about why another person would say or do what they said or did, or assuming someone has knowledge that they don't have, a simple conversation can often clear up a misunderstanding and any grievance previously held can be dropped.

We don't know what goes on in another's life. We don't know what might have caused a particular emotion or strong reaction. We don't always know what is important to others. We don't know how they've been taught, or how they've learned to survive, in a particular situation.

Have you ever read a book or watched a film where the main character, the one you relate to, is a crook? Of course you have. Have you ever found yourself wishing the character success in their purpose, whether it be stealing the money, exacting revenge or getting away with a deed the like of which you yourself would never attempt? If you have then you are, just for a moment, getting caught up in their story, where they convince themselves it's ok to steal, cheat, lie or even kill. Are you guilty? No, you just observed. Have you empathised with someone, albeit a fictional character, and therefore can see a way to excuse their guilt? Maybe.

Is it you or could it be me?

I might think negatively about someone else when they behave in a way that, to my mind, isn't loving. They do or say something that I consider to be unkind, proud, rude, untrue or unjust. They don't see things the way I do, they don't believe what I believe.

Maybe someone has said something that has hurt or offended me, that has caused me to think negatively about that person. When I am able to step back and look objectively on the situation, I might see that I was being over-sensitive, or that the words hurt because, deep down, I knew there was some validity in what the person was saying.

Often we can be sensitive about being "wronged" because the behaviour of others resonates with something within us. If I call someone stubborn and argumentative then could it not be that I also have a tendency to be stubborn and argumentative? If I complain because someone talks too much, or always wants the limelight, could it be that I like to talk a lot and I like the limelight? If I'm working with someone and I find them controlling and set in their ways, could it be that I'm controlling and set in my ways?

It's precisely those things that upset us the most that tend to be reflections of ourselves, especially when the thought is a painful one, no matter how vehemently we may wish to deny the possibility. What would be helpful is some honest self-reflection.

Winning an argument

What about those times when I'm in an argument with someone and they're driving me mad because they can't see that I'm right?

Arguments, or differences of opinion, are often at the root of on-going unforgiveness. People can fall out and never speak again over the silliest of disagreements.

Should I just back down every time, for the sake of peace and an easy life?

First of all, I think I'm right, but so do they. Not only that but they think I'm wrong. How could they think I'm wrong? If I look past the desire to be right, I might be able to see that there could be more than one way of looking at this issue.

If I can lose the belief in there always being one right and one wrong way to look at something, and accept that, to some degree at least, we can both be right, this will help my acceptance of the situation.

Secondly, the real reason for my upset is often hidden, sometimes underneath layers of beliefs and assumptions. If I can examine my reaction to the situation, and ask myself some searching questions, maybe I can be honest with myself about what might be at the root of it.

Is there some reason why I might actually want there to be a rift between us? Might I have something to gain from being able to say they pushed me away, rather than that I pushed them away, which may or may not be closer to the truth?

Thirdly, if I can accept that we learn most when we're in an uncomfortable situation, a disagreement that has pressed all my buttons could be a great learning opportunity.

In order to move forward I need to see things differently. I'd like it if they did too, but I can't determine that. The best way is to say "Okay, Holy Spirit, show me a different way to look at this situation". In my case it's often a last resort, when something has bugged me for a while, and I know I would be happier and live a more peaceful life if I asked the question sooner.

Agreeing to disagree

I have my truth, others have theirs. Sometimes we have to accept that, just as I'm struggling to see something their way, they can't see it my way either.

It can be that I not only want to win the argument and get my own way, I want the other person, and anyone else I choose to talk to about the issue, to agree with me wholeheartedly. Thinking that someone doesn't see things exactly as I do jars me, leaves me dissatisfied. I bring to mind every justification for my opinion, digging myself deeper and deeper into my trench.

Having someone think anything less than well of me upsets my ego. Is my ego a bit fragile? Maybe if I had better self-esteem or confidence then I'd be more comfortable with having someone else think I'm wrong.

Am I looking for approval from the people around me? Why do I need anyone else's approval? If I am listening to God as to what is right for me then I should see no need to seek approval from anyone else, just as nobody around me needs my approval when they feel they're being led a different way to me.

Agreeing to disagree means accepting that not everyone will agree with me on every subject throughout my life. I just have to know my truth and not try to force it on others. I have to accept that their view can be different and still be their truth.

Forgiving the unforgivable

The deeper, more painful hurts are far harder to rationalise and therefore much harder to forgive. If someone has knowingly, deliberately, hurt you or someone you love, then you can't pass that off as a misunderstanding, or satisfy yourself with seeing things from their point of view.

Would God forgive anything? I think the answer is yes. Therefore we should forgive anything. Even the most heinous crime, committed against us or our loved ones.

There are some wonderful stories of forgiveness told by holocaust survivors (for example Eva Korr and Edith Eger). They are mind-blowing. How can someone forgive individuals who caused untold suffering, on a personal and global level? The answer is they forgave because they realised it was the only way that they could achieve peace of mind. The same is true for any of us, with any grievance.

Therefore we are being called to forgive without the benefit of understanding why. Maybe that's the point. Maybe the lesson is in letting go of a grievance, simply because to let go is the right thing to do, with no need and no ability to understand why things happened as they did.

Most of the forgiveness examples I can think of hinge on the fact that a judgement has been made against a person for something where the person is likely to be unaware of the consequences, either completely or in part.

This covers all manner of misunderstandings, and cases where excessive aggression has been used. It can also cover selfish acts, such as leaving a restaurant without paying – if you've ever worked in a restaurant kitchen or waiting tables surely that would make you less likely to do this.

Abhorrent crimes must surely be the result of a lack of empathy. I knew someone who'd once interviewed a paedophile, within the context of a therapy session, and had been astounded that the perpetrator said of his victims "they can always get therapy when they're older". If he had any inkling of the depth of suffering his actions had caused, I wonder if he would have stopped himself sooner.

The doctors who worked for Josef Mengele must have known what they were doing was evil, surely? Or did they? They'd been brainwashed into thinking that one race of people could be inferior to another to the point of being unworthy of consideration, however absurd that sounds to us now. Just like the hunters that kill purely for the prize, they had no empathy with their victims.

Unforgiveness is a defence mechanism. It says "I'm right, you're wrong, I'm going to protect myself from you so that you can't hurt me again". Yet instead of leaving me protected, it leaves me vulnerable. It block's God's love. It gives power to the person, or the event. For as long as the grievance is felt, that person has a hold over me and affects the way I respond in certain situations. If I manage to let go of the grievance, through forgiveness, I am freeing myself from that hold. It's not about the other person. We're not letting them off the hook, or condoning any particular behaviour, we're saying, "this happened, I'm letting go of it, it's in the past, I'm choosing not to let it hurt me anymore".

There are people who are violent and pose a risk to those around them and I'm not suggesting we ignore that risk. There are people who need to be incarcerated, for the protection of society as a whole. I believe these people can still be forgiven, however.

Having forgiven someone, we don't need to necessarily be their best friend. What we want to get to us a place where we can let go of the grievance and where thoughts of them or whatever they did don't leave us feeling so angry or upset. We need to take the sting out. Once the sting is removed we can be around them or not, that's our choice.

Forgiveness is a process, it might not happen all at once. In going through that process we might learn more about ourselves and our sensitivities, or aspects of our own feelings of guilt. Just as we can project our feelings of anger onto another, so we can project unresolved feelings of our own guilt.

Add love to the mix

Whenever there's an exchange between people that is unloving, such as an argument, then the only way to move forward is for love to be added to the exchange. Love comes in the form of forgiveness.

For example, my daughters came back from an afternoon at the park with their friends, upset at having been accused of being intimidating to a couple of younger girls. The mother of one of the girls challenged them, and was very angry and verbally abusive towards them. There was much upset at the accusation, and particularly at the way it was put across. When I was told about it I considered my response.

My first instinct was to find out who the woman was that had used apparently foul language and threatening behaviour against teenagers. This was no way for her to behave. What example was she setting and what did she hope to achieve by being so aggressive? I'd find a way of identifying her and approach her with an accusatory stance "Nobody speaks to my daughters like that!"

What would this achieve? This would be a continuation of bad behaviour. I would be descending to her level. She would get confirmation of her perception that these girls are trouble "See, look at the mother!"

A calmer approach would be to adopt a more measured and reasonable stance. "I know a group of teenagers can look menacing, particularly when most of them look older than they are, but if you knew them you'd know they're not bad girls and I really don't think there was any need to swear at them like that."

I liked this idea better. The only trouble is she might carry on in the same vein with me, convinced she was in the right. The argument might continue, like a tennis match, each trying to counter with a stronger, more emotional return.

Then I paused to ask myself what would Jesus do? I don't think Jesus would get into a slanging match. I think Jesus would see inside the person, recognise the fears that must surely be at the root of such anger and I think he would tell this woman she's loved and she has nothing to fear.

I therefore believe my job in this interaction is a simple one. If I was to talk to her, I'd not enter into an argument with her. I wouldn't tell her what is ok and not ok to do, nor would I talk to her about the love of God that protects her, which she might or might not want to hear. I'm simply going to forgive her. I'm not going to tell her I forgive her, that could be sanctimonious and condescending. I'm just going to treat her as a reasonable person and hope that in doing so any defences she might still be wanting to put up can be taken down.

Part of this feels uncomfortably passive, like I'm giving in. I have a need to protect my daughters and this pulls at a cord within me. However, I know my girls are looked after. I know that, whilst this interaction was a painful one, it was necessary for them to learn that not everybody sees you the way you see yourself. It's also important to learn that the right response to an aggressive person is not more aggression. Someone needs to add love to the mix, that's the only way it can be resolved.

Love keeps no record of wrongs

There are ways of partially forgiving someone. Saying "you were wrong but I'll let you off this time" isn't true forgiveness. Keeping a record of the "wrong" means you can bring it out of the cupboard and wave it around at any time in the future. It has to be true forgiveness, true letting go.

In order to totally let go of unforgiveness, I may need to first ask God to show me how to perceive of a situation differently. Let me see the situation with fresh eyes, see it as God sees it, because God sees it and forgives.

Forgiveness in a "woke" culture

We are in a "cancel culture", where people can be frozen out for expressing opinions that are not "woke", ie for expressing a view that is deemed as unsympathetic to a section of society.

In a culture such as this unforgiveness abounds. Who is right? Are we right to chastise and write off a person for views they hold or might have expressed in the past? If we choose to ignore views we don't share, could it be that we're condoning them?

It is my belief that whilst we can judge a comment or an action to be unfair, unsympathetic, or otherwise unloving, we should not judge the person. Judging another person puts us as no better than the person we are judging.

Do we need our celebrities to be perfect? If so we're likely to be more disappointed the more we find out about them. Nobody is perfect, but because someone might have a view I don't share doesn't mean they aren't good actors, musicians, authors, or whatever.

This issue is further compounded by our tendency to, literally, put people on a pedestal. Commemorating the life of a person who has made some significant contribution to history is not a declaration of their perfection, it is recognition of the fact that something they did was worthy of being remembered. Our perceptions change over time, and awareness of their human failings might make us less likely to deify them as we once did. They can, understandably, become to be seen as epitomes of wrongdoing rather than exemplars of good deeds.

We are all equal in God's eyes. All the credit, for what is achieved through us, should go to God.

Therefore I believe we should neither condemn nor glorify each other, neither put people on pedestals nor write them off as villains for views we don't share, rather we should respect and forgive each other, always.

Letting go

I believe that all the things that happen to us teach us something about life and about ourselves, if we let them. Maybe sometimes the lesson can seem too hard and too painful. What other people are able to learn is a matter for them and not for me. I can only do what I believe is right for me.

There can be no valid reason for lack of forgiveness. Not even for the most unthinkable wrongdoing. Being sure that we are right is not a justification for holding on to a grievance. Holding on does nothing to affect the person we aren't forgiving, it affects us. It is bad for us and our relationship with God.

Letting go enables us to relax. Letting go allows us to open the doors in our mind that we've wanted to keep tightly shut. Letting go allows God into every situation. Letting go enables healing.

I believe love is the answer, and love, where there has been a lack of love, is forgiveness.

The tense used in the verb "forgive" in Matthew's account gives a sense of "we should", ie "we should forgive others". It's as if we're giving ourselves the command.

In terms of the definition of our "contract" with God, so far we've said that God gives us our daily bread and forgives us our trespasses. For our part, we've seen that we need to carry out God's will and here we pledge to forgive others as God forgives us.

We should let go of unforgiveness in the same way.
62

Lead Us not into Temptation

Καὶ μὴ εἰσενέγκῃς ἡμᾶς εἰς πειρασμόν
Kai me eisenenkes hemas eis peirasmon
And not lead us into temptation

This is the same in Matthew as in Luke.

The verb "lead us" isn't quite the same tense as the other verbs, but when used with a negative, "lead us not", it effectively becomes the same.

We are either asking God to do something God would never do, or we must look for another explanation.

The amended translation, requested by the Pope, is "do not let us be led". The justification, I imagine, is to recognise that whatever leads us into temptation, it isn't God. Therefore "do not let us be led" is implying a stronger resistance to temptation, rather than an absence of temptation. The New Living Translation agrees: "Don't let us yield to temptation".

If this were the only instance in the prayer of effectively asking God to do what God would/wouldn't do, then I'd me more likely to agree the translation "do not let us be led". However, I think another way of looking at it is that it is defining what God does, rather than making a request.

God, you do not lead us into temptation.

Temptation is a menace. Temptation is something that's bad for us wrapped up as something appealing. It depends on your own particular weakness. It could be a beer or a glass of wine, a cigarette, a piece of chocolate cake, a line of cocaine, a flirtatious smile, a website, lovely things to buy, the urge to place a bet, whatever. The point is that it's something you find hard to resist that you know ultimately will lead you to no good. What we're asking for is help to overcome the temptation and walk away.

We need to recognise the difference between the thrill of the thing that tempts us and the "inner no" that recognises this as something that is ultimately not good for us.

The point is that if we stick with God, and with our "inner yes", we won't go the way of temptation.

Jesus is saying "you may be tempted, but you don't have to give in to it". To be tempted is not the issue, and we shouldn't feel guilty about it. Temptation is all around, and will always be. The point is that if we want to avoid temptation as much as possible, we stick with God.

Whatever it is that would lead us the wrong way, the way that is not helpful to our purpose and our calling, it's not God.

It is not You that leads us into temptation.

But Deliver Us from Evil

> Ἀλλὰ ῥῦσαι ἡμᾶς ἀπὸ τοῦ πονηροῦ
> Alla rusai hemas apo tou ponerou
> But deliver us from evil

This line is in Matthew's account only.

Not only do we know that God will show us how to stay away from things that would harm us, we also know that whenever we end up in a bad place – physically, mentally or emotionally – we just need to call out to God and we'll be back on track.

Like the line above, this is about our direction in life. At any crossroads we can go the way that is right by God, or the way that isn't. If we believe in a God that has our best interests at heart then we must go the way we feel God is leading us all the time. Every decision, even minor ones, should be given to God. God knows what is right for us and what isn't.

Bad things are out there, but we mustn't worry about ending up on the wrong side of the tracks. If we worry about avoiding evil then we could end up being worried about going anywhere. Evil isn't to be feared. God will deliver us back safely if we find ourselves where we shouldn't be. When the "inner no" is screaming to us that, though this looked like the right path, it plainly isn't, we just call to God and we find our way to "inner yes".

If we are to achieve whatever it is that God has planned for us, there will be times when we need to be brave. If we sit around waiting to be absolutely positive every time we think of doing something, we might end up stuck, frozen in the headlights. If we know that a wrong turn does not mean the end, we can plough ahead, secure in the knowledge that if this way turns out to be the wrong way, we'll know about it sooner or later and we'll be able to get back to where we ought to be.

How do we get back to where we need to be? By developing our listening skills, by interpreting the "inner no" and being able to find the thing that gives us the "inner yes". This, like the line before us, is about guidance through life. When we stick with our Heavenly Father we can always get back on track, and we'll be forgiven for having gone the wrong way.

The last few lines go together, all being about direction. You forgive us when we go wrong, you don't lead us the wrong way, you put us back on course. Put this together with "We want to carry out Your will" and we have the full picture. Let us refer to You when we set up our navigation system, You help us define where we're going, You tell us how to get there ("at the end of the road turn right") and You tell us when we've taken a wrong turn ("turn around when possible").

But You bring us back when we go wrong.

For Thine is the Kingdom

> Ὅτι σοῦ ἐστιν ἡ βασιλεία
> Hoti sou estin he basileia
> For yours is the kingdom

This section isn't included in all version of the Lord's Prayer, and recent translations of Matthew and Luke omit it, as most scholars feel it was never part of the original texts. It is commonly added to the protestant version of the Lord's Prayer, and is consistent with other advice on prayer, such as in 1 Chronicles 29:11.

It rounds the prayer off with a certain symmetry, echoing the nature of God as referenced at the beginning of the prayer.

We start the Lord's Prayer by saying "Your kingdom come", and at the end we say "Yours is the kingdom". If "Your kingdom" meant heaven, as discussed earlier, then "Yours is the kingdom" is a reminder that the kingdom of heaven belongs to God.

In the time of the New Testament there was a distinction between heaven ("up there") and earth, where we are. Now that we know we are a planet that exists within the universe, we might lose that distinction and say that everything is God's, everything in the whole of the universe.

Back in the time of Jesus, when the earth was thought to be flat and the heavens were something separate, set apart from the land. The distinction between earth and heaven was a question of opposites, rather than earth being part of the universe, or "the heavens". Here we have a different concept – that God's kingdom is "up there", and we want God's kingdom to manifest on earth. The inference, I believe, is that earth, whilst created by God, is not God's domain. This echoes references elsewhere that we should be in the world but "not belong to the world"[10].

If earth isn't God's domain then what is it?

The physical realm relates to everything we can see, hear, smell, touch and taste. The spiritual realm is where God is. The spiritual realm is what gives life and inspires creativity.

We want us and everyone around us to be happy, healthy, peaceful and to shine with love. We want more of God in everything.

"The world", as it's often referred to, is where the problems are. The world contains beauty, love and much that is divinely inspired, but it also contains those things that come from a lack of love, those things that come from man without God.

Materialism, competitiveness, selfishness, desire for power and control all relate to the world. There is much fear of the threats that exist in the world, and that fear feeds our anger and our wars.

---

[10] John 17:14

If we want improvements in our life, we look to Heaven. Heaven is devoid of all the negative things that blight the world. Heaven belongs to God.

Heaven is Yours.

The Power

> καὶ ἡ δύναμις
> kai he dunamis
> and the power

The power is God's. What do we mean by power? Strength, ability, force, energy? God is where we came from and God is the source of all creativity.

If we think of power in the form of electricity then electricity needs an appliance in order to have a function. A house with electric sockets has the ability to have lights that shine, ovens that cook and a television that streams entertainment. Without the appliances it does nothing, it just has potential.

What are the appliances for God's power? We are. We have the ability to plug ourselves in and do amazing things. We can sing, dance, create, heal. We can love, we can radiate happiness, we can literally shine.

We don't always shine, not all of the time. What happens is that we come unplugged, or we turn down the brightness, by focusing our attention in the wrong place. We have anxieties, fears, anger, unforgiveness, and all these things diminish our light.

God's is the power, but the power works in and through us. We are necessary for God's power to be apparent in the world. This is the purpose of life. We just need to "allow" God, let God do what God does.

The Power

When we align with God, when we seek to follow the path that is right for us, the unique path for us as an individual, we access God's power. Everybody does it, whether they know it or not. Musicians, artists, writers, poets, teachers, doctors, nurses, therapists, lawyers, computer programmers, chefs, gardeners, builders, carpenters, shop workers, those in positions of power and influence, everyone has the ability to tap into and express God's power. In some it is more obvious than in others, such as those whose work obviously relies on creativity, but everyone, even pencil-pushers in lowly office jobs, or anyone doing repetitive manual work, everyone has the potential to express God's power, in every aspect of life. It is what gives inspiration and generates success.

What if I'm not aligned with what God wants me to do? How will I know? You'll feel an "inner no". You'll become aware that you're doing your job simply for the money and enduring it rather than enjoying it. Or you're doing something to fit in with somebody else's agenda and that just doesn't feel right. There are options, there are always options. The right option enables God's power to shine through us.

The power that we get from God is the power for good – to give, to create, to heal, to love. It is limitless, immeasurable, unimaginable in scale.

The power to do anything is Yours

And the Glory

κ αὶ ἡ δόξα
kai he doxa
and the glory

The word used is doxa, which has a sense of "opinion" or "reputation". Another way of expressing it might be to say "you take the credit".

This is perhaps a reminder to keep humble. When we are aligned with our true purpose and achieving great things, the power is God's, and we must remember that. If we get carried away, thinking about how well we're doing and how invincible we are, we might become proud and lose the connection we have with God, as the source of our greatness.

The word doxa is rarely used in a negative sense, ie a poor opinion or bad reputation. Therefore it doesn't mean that God is to blame for all the bad stuff, or when we don't have the success we think we might deserve.

When things go well, we should thank God. When things go badly, we should look to our connection with God, not in the sense of looking for blame, but simply to ask where we should go from here. Whatever scrape we might be in, God can help us move forward in the right way. Then, by being aligned to God, we can allow more of His power through us.

If we think of ourselves as electrical appliances that God brings to life and uses for good, then the arms, legs and head might be ours, but the power is Gods. Likewise the credit, for what we achieve, is God's.

All the credit, for what is achieved through us, goes to You.

For ever and ever, Amen

> εἰς τοὺς αἰῶνας, Ἀμήν
> eis tous aionas, Amen
> For the ages, Amen

This is the way things are and the way things will always be. This hints at the timeless nature of God, God has always been there and always will be.

This is what we pray together.

> *This always has been and always will be the case*

> *We say this prayer together.*

Living the Lord's Prayer

Taking the essence of the prayer, then, we have a contract with God as follows:

- God gives us the sustenance we need.
- God guides us the right way and redirects us when we go wrong.
- God forgives.

We, for our part need to:

- Always forgive.
- Give the credit to God.
- Keep close to God so that we can establish and carry out God's will as much as we can.

Prayer, then, could be seen as a reminder and a thank you for what God does for us, and a prompt to ourselves of what we need to do.

To be most effective it should be constant, throughout the day, whenever there's a decision to be made, rather than reserved for specific daily or weekly time slots. It's about living in a Lord's Prayer mindset.

Sustenance

If I remember that God always gives me the sustenance I need then why should I worry about not having enough of anything? This means enough food to eat, money to pay my bills, anything that I need to keep me sustained.

If I trust in God for the things God does for me then I have no need to be afraid, surely?

The extent to which I can be free from anxiety is the same as the extent to which I can allow God into any situation. If I had sufficient faith in my connection with God, I could be confident in the face of any difficulty.

I need to train my mind to always trust God for anything I need.

Guidance

I no longer see asking for guidance as a defined activity that is separate from everyday life, I see it as an integral part of everything I do.

Whenever there's anything I want to achieve, I should ask God what I can do to make that thing happen. It makes me think of the joke where the man is stranded in the desert and refuses help from a passing stranger with a camel, then another with a jeep, then a biplane, saying "the Lord will save me", only to die and to be told "I sent you a camel, a jeep and a plane, what more did you want?"

Living the Lord's Prayer doesn't mean a life free of challenges or problems, it means that I know where to look whenever I feel bogged down. That help might come in the form of understanding the need to accept a difficult situation, or to stop resisting the inevitable, or it could be a flashing neon light pointing to the way forward.

God speaks to us all the time and helps us all the time, we just have to hear what we're being told, and act on it.

There's a prayer that is often quoted as a good way to start each day: "Where would you have me go? What would you have me do? What would you have me say, and to whom?" [11]

I need to remember that the better I can tune into what God is trying to tell me, the greater success I'll have in anything that I'm trying to do. I need to stop trying to control everything on my own and accept that God sees everything and God can guide me the right way.

Trusting God with decisions in life can take a surprising amount of bravery, on those occasions when the way I feel guided is against the flow of those around me. We all tend to be herding creatures, more comfortable when we're going along with everyone else, and stepping out alone, in whatever context, can be challenging. If I'm sufficiently confident that this is the right way for me, regardless of whether it's the right way for those around me, I need have nothing to fear.

I need to train my mind to always remember to ask for guidance.

Asking for forgiveness

---

[11] Quote taken from https://www.oprah.com/spirit/how-to-be-spiritually-fit-marianne-williamson

I know that any time I become aware that I got it wrong I am forgiven. I just need to be open to the possibility that I might need to change direction.

I make mistakes on a regular basis. What changes as I go through life is not necessarily that the mistakes are fewer, but that I believe I recognise them sooner. If God can forgive me for this then I must forgive myself.

Do I need to ask a priest or other minister for forgiveness? Does forgiveness need to be given in a church setting?

I don't think so. There might be times when I find it helpful to talk something through with another person, to work out where it is that I'm going wrong, but it's not my belief that a particular ritual is required before I'm granted forgiveness.

I've tended to feel a bit uncomfortable with that part of a church service where we're prompted to ask for forgiveness for those things which we ought not to have done, or for not doing those things which we ought to have done. I struggled with this before studying the Lord's Prayer, and now I'm closer to understanding why.

God forgives. We just have to acknowledge that we got it wrong and our forgiveness is guaranteed. Therefore it's not about making time to sit and reflect on what we might already know we didn't do so well, rather it's about recognising, in any moment, the need to change direction.

Time spent on self-reflection is a good thing, but a regular time slot where we list the ways in which we've not been good enough isn't, I believe, helpful, and could potentially serve to reinforce a feeling of guilt and inadequacy.

I think most of us carry around a weight of unexplained guilt. We may not even be aware of it, but it shapes us, and finding a way to free ourselves from it will make us far more capable of achieving our potential.

We might value being told by a minister or a priest that we are forgiven, so that we can truly lose the feeling of guilt. This, to me, is a *reminder* that we are forgiven, rather than a question of being told "*now* you are forgiven".

I need to remember that I'm forgiven and I don't need to carry around a burden of guilt.

Forgiving others

Let me always forgive. Any time I'm holding on to a grievance I need to bring it to mind and let it go. I may need to ask to see it differently, see it as God sees it, so that it no longer has any hold on me.

God just wants us to be the best that we can be. He wants us to heal our rifts with others and live together in harmony. I think it's more useful if, instead of having a regular slot where we draw to mind everything we need forgiveness for, we make time to reflect on what *we* haven't forgiven *others* for, and to ask for new light to be shed on these things, to enable us to move forward together.

I see the unravelling of unforgiveness as a lifetime's journey. Being aware of the benefits of, or necessity for, forgiveness is different from being able to truly achieve that forgiveness, which may take a good deal of work.

Personally, despite a keenness to forgive, I seem to bounce along from judgement to judgement. I tend to see the same kind of issues coming round again, like a very slow merry-go-round. Whenever I find myself in a situation where someone has annoyed or upset me, if I look beyond the specifics of this instance, I find a recognisable pattern that I've seen before.

The truth is I'm seeing an aspect of myself reflected back at me. In order to fully understand myself I need to strip away the emotion and find the defining thoughts that are triggering my response. Could it be my own perceived guilt that I see reflected in someone else?

I need to train my mind to understand what my reaction to others tells me about myself, rather than judging others.

Being grateful

I need to remember what God does for me. I need to get away from thinking of those things I don't have and remember everything I do have.

I need to train my mind to be grateful for everything I have, everything I am, all the people I interact with, and for all that we can achieve together if we'd just allow more of our loving God into our lives.

Asking God

Whilst I'm suggesting My Lord's Prayer isn't specifically about asking for help, that doesn't mean I don't believe we should ask God for help. Quite the reverse. I believe God is always ready and waiting to be involved, and the more we involve God, the more success we'll have in anything. I need to remember that asking for help, like asking for guidance, should be a first port of call rather than a last resort.

I believe that the energy or the thought process around the request makes a lot of difference. "Please can I...because I don't have..." has an energy of lack, whereas "Please can I...because I know you can help me" has an energy of grateful anticipation.

The power of positive thinking would be easy to underestimate. When I want something to happen I think about it, ask God to help me, feel the happiness that comes from remembering God is always on hand, and then leave the request with God.

If I'm struggling with a heavy burden in my life, it's as if I'm walking along while carrying a shopping bag full of books. The weight slows me down and can prove difficult to manage. When I ask God to help me, I need to let go of the handles of the bag. In my anxiety I can be reluctant to take my hands away, but if I've given it to

God then I need to truly let go, and enjoy the fact that I no longer have the burden any more.

I need to train my mind to always ask, and to do so in a positive, grateful and confident manner.

It's easier said than done, but I believe that if we always remember how close God is to us, and how much help is at hand, we can achieve so much more than if we plough on thinking we're alone.

We all have a part to play in our combined future. We might think of ourselves and our abilities as of no great significance, but we are the appliances for God's power, and if we all plug ourselves in and allow that power to course through us, we can transform the world.

My Lord's Prayer

Giver of life to us all.

Where Heaven is You are.

We call Your Holy name.

Let us draw near to You.

We want to carry out Your will.

It is You that gives us the sustenance we need each day.

You forgive us when we go wrong. You set us free from our guilt.

We should let go of unforgiveness in the same way.

It is not You that leads us into temptation.

But You bring us back when we go wrong.

Heaven is Yours.

The power to do anything is Yours.

All the credit, for what is achieved through us, goes to You.

This always has been and always will be the case

We say this prayer together.

Appendix: Further Notes on Grammar

In order to analyse the verbs within Lord's Prayer, there are certain points to consider.

A verb can be described as having the following:

> Tense (past, present, future)
>
> *He does, he did, he will do*
>
> Mood (indicative, subjunctive, imperative)
>
> *You sing, you would sing, Sing!*
>
> Person (first, second, third), singular or plural
>
> *I/we, you, he/she/they*
>
> Voice (active, passive, middle)
>
> *I kick, I am kicked, I kick myself*

Tense

There are 2 tenses used within the Lord's Prayer. In "Thine is the kingdom", the word "is" uses the *present* tense, all other verbs are in the prayer are *aorist* tense.

The aorist tense is a past tense, when in the indicative mood, but becomes a command when in the imperative mood. The aorist imperative means "do (something) now", with a sense of urgency, or a need for an action to be completed. This is as opposed to a present imperative, which would have a sense of "keep on doing". It seems odd to consider a past tense as being a command or request. I like to think of it as an American might say "do it already!"

Mood

Most verbs in the Lord's Prayer are *imperative*:

> <u>Hallowed</u> (be thy name)
>
> (Your kingdom) <u>come</u>
>
> (Your will) <u>be done</u>
>
> <u>Give</u> (us this day)
>
> <u>Forgive</u> (us)
>
> <u>Deliver</u> (us)

However there are 3 exceptions:

> Thine <u>is</u> (the kingdom) = present *indicative*
> This is a statement of fact.

> We <u>forgive</u> = aorist *indicative*
> This has a sense of something we should be doing.

> <u>Lead</u> (us not) = aorist *subjunctive*
>
> > The aorist subjunctive, when combined with a negative (lead us not) can either have a sense of "you should not" or it can be a negative command, along the same lines as the aorist imperative, hence "lead us not".

Taking tense and mood, we effectively have a list of commands. In being aorist imperative there is a sense of "do it now", and a sense of the action needing to be completed, rather than "do this and keep on doing it".

Person

Those that are in the *second* person are all aorist imperative, which means we are telling God to:

> Give us our daily bread
>
> Forgive us our trespasses
>
> Lead us not into temptation
>
> Deliver us from evil.

There are also several verbs in the *third* person.

One is a statement of fact, using the present indicative:

> Thine is the kingdom.

One is an instruction, using the aorist:

> Thy kingdom come.

Then there is the instruction for us:

> We forgive = aorist indicative
> This has a sense of something we should be doing.

Voice

All the verbs are *active* except for two which are *passive*:

> Hallowed be thy name
>
> Thy will be done.

The prayer is that these should "be done". By whom?

If God isn't the one doing them, since they're not in the second person ("you"), then it must be someone else: us, or, possibly, something we achieve together.

A Prayer of Thanks?

Does the grammar give us any room to consider this as a prayer of thanks rather than requests?

Given that the tense is a past tense, if the mood could be interpreted as *indicative* rather than *imperative* then we would have:

> You gave us our daily bread
>
> You forgave us our trespasses
>
> You led us not into temptation
>
> You delivered us from evil

However the inference would be that these actions happened in the past and have been completed.

Alternatively, interpreting the verbs as present indicative we would have:

> You give us our daily bread
>
> You forgive us our trespasses
>
> You lead us not into temptation
>
> You deliver us from evil.

This has a timeless quality, which I believe to be appropriate. I think that, given the context, there's something to recommend it.

Time is, I think, an important point to consider. When do we pray for? Now, or for some time in the future? I think that prayers are all for now. The future is a set of endless opportunities, the past has gone, we pray for now.

The Greek of the bible wasn't as refined as you might think, and it's hard to pick up subtleties of expression. the The Classical Greek of the bible is far more complex than Ancient Greek, and I think in summary that context is the most important factor.

Rather than represent the aorist imperatives within the prayer as requests, I prefer to use the present indicative, which makes the prayer more about a statement of fact, an expression of gratitude, or a reminder to ourselves, than a request.

<u>About the Author</u>

Jean Webb studied Ancient Greek at Canon Slade School, Bolton, and then at Birmingham University as part of a combined honours degree in Maths and Ancient Greek, in the late 1980s.

After a career in IT, she now practices as a holistic therapist, and enjoys writing, painting and exploring all aspects of spirituality.

She lives in Oxfordshire with her family.

www.ingramcontent.com/pod-product-compliance
Lightning Source LLC
Chambersburg PA
CBHW022116050726
47591CB00002B/813